See It Through

Merie Vision Publishing, LLC
www.merievisionpublishing.com

ISBN: 978-1-961213-30-2
Library of Congress Control Number on record

First Print Edition: June 2024

Love
in its
purest
Forms

Love
in its
purest
Forms

Dada, why do you love me tons?

I love how your little feet runs.

I love your cute little Afro buns.

I love when you're done eating and you say, "All done!"

Dada, why do you love me tons?

I love when we play out in the sun.

I love when we play soccer, and you scream, "I'm numba ONE!!"

I love when your
face lights up when
I call you "Hun."

Dada, why do you love me tons?

I love how you just always want to have fun.

I love when you
show me your
"wittle" guns.

I love how
adventurous you
are, and you fear
none.

You want to know
why Dada loves
you tons?

Just know, it's
because with you,
my baby girl, I feel
I have won!!

www.ingramcontent.com/pod-product-compliance
Lightning Source LLC
Chambersburg PA
CBHW041531120626
46551CB00018B/2650